# Going Ice Fishing

## Lever vs. Screw

by Mari Schuh

Lerner Publications ◆ Minneapolis

**LERNER**

**SOURCE**

Expand learning beyond the printed book. Download free, complementary educational resources for this book from our website, www.lernersource.com.

Copyright © 2016 by Lerner Publishing Group, Inc.

All rights reserved. International copyright secured. No part of this book may be reproduced, stored in a retrieval system, or transmitted in any form or by any means—electronic, mechanical, photocopying, recording, or otherwise—without the prior written permission of Lerner Publishing Group, Inc., except for the inclusion of brief quotations in an acknowledged review.

All images in this book are used with the permission of: © Todd Strand/Independent Picture Service except: © Louella938/Shutterstock.com, p. 7 (top left); © iStockphoto.com/FreezeFrameStudio, p. 7 (bottom left); © iStockphoto.com/vovan13, p. 7 (top right); © iStockphoto.com/eagleotter, p. 13; © afitz/Shutterstock.com, p. 14; © Ann Murie/Dreamstime.com, p. 15.

Front cover: © Todd Strand/Independent Picture Service.

Main body text set in ITC Avant Garde Gothic Std Medium 21/25.
Typeface provided by Adobe Systems.

Lerner Publications Company
A division of Lerner Publishing Group, Inc.
241 First Avenue North
Minneapolis, MN 55401 USA

For reading levels and more information, look up this title at www.lernerbooks.com.

Library of Congress Cataloging-in-Publication Data

Schuh, Mari C., 1975–
    Going ice fishing : lever vs. screw / by Mari Schuh.
        pages cm. — (First step nonfiction. Simple machines to the rescue)
    Includes index.
        ISBN 978-1-4677-8029-2 (lb : alk. paper) — ISBN 978-1-4677-8300-2 (pb : alk. paper) — ISBN 978-1-4677-8301-9 (eb pdf)
    1. Levers—Juvenile literature. 2. Augers—Juvenile literature. 3. Screws—Juvenile literature. 4. Ice fishing—Juvenile literature. I. Title.
TJ147.S418 2016
621.8—dc23                                                            2015000259

Manufactured in the United States of America
1 – CG – 7/15/15

*Easy*
*J*
*Schuh*
*Main*

# Table of Contents

Getting Ready                        4

Sofia Uses a Lever                   8

Diego Uses a Screw                  12

Diego Makes a Hole                  20

Glossary                            23

Index                               24

Sofia and her uncle Diego are going ice fishing.

They need to make a hole
in the ice. What can help
them?                                    5

They have a snow shovel.
They have an ice **auger** too.

These are kinds of simple machines.

Both tools are **simple machines**.

Sofia tries the shovel.

A lever is a type of simple machine.

The shovel's handle is a **lever**. A lever can lift objects.

9

The shovel helps. It lifts the snow.

But the shovel cannot make
a hole in the ice.

# Diego Uses a Screw

Diego uses the ice auger. An auger is a type of **screw**.

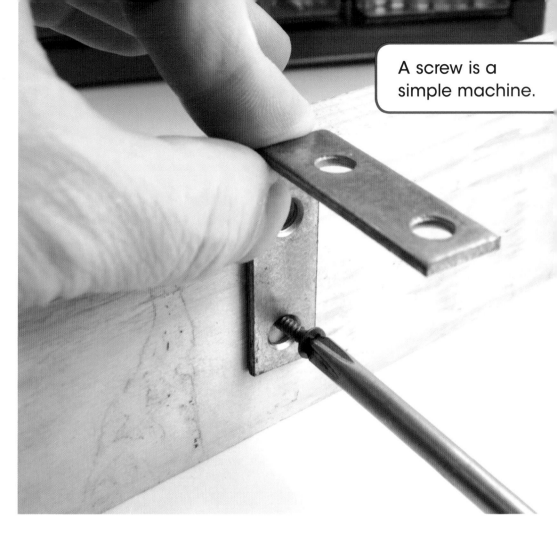

A screw is a simple machine.

Screws hold objects together.

This screw makes a hole in wood.

Screws also make holes in objects.

14

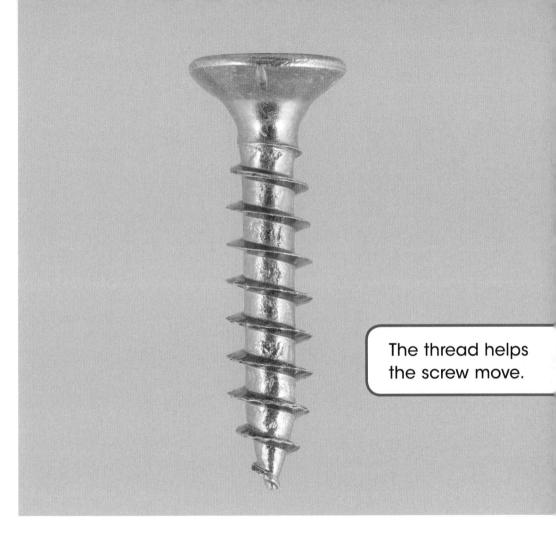

The thread helps the screw move.

A screw has a rod and a **thread**. The thread wraps around the rod. 15

An auger's blade is the
thread of the screw.

Diego turns the auger's handle.

The auger's blade turns.

The blade cuts into the ice.

# Diego Makes a Hole

The blade makes a hole.

Sofia and Diego can go ice fishing!

How can you use screws?

# Glossary

**auger** – a spiral-shaped tool often used for making holes

**lever** – a bar that rests and turns on a fixed point

**screw** – a rod with a thread wrapped around it

**simple machines** – machines with one moving part or no moving parts

**thread** – the sharp ridge that wraps around a screw

# Index

ice auger – 6, 12, 16–18

lever – 9

rod – 15

screw – 12–16, 22

shovel – 6, 8–11

simple machines – 7

thread – 15–16